Wannabe
An Explorer

Philip Steele

PARRAGON

THE GREAT OUTDOORS

All explorers must make a start somewhere. Even if you live in a city, you can probably reach the countryside by bus or train. You may even be able to reach a national park, where there are mountains or lakes. These are often places where serious explorers and mountain climbers train before leaving on an expedition. Young people should only go hiking or backpacking with trained leaders.

SAFETY FIRST
Good explorers plan their route carefully before they start.
They let other people know the route they are following, in case of accidents and they take the right equipment.
They are also prepared for any accidents that might happen.

A day pack should contain spare clothing, food, a hot drink in a flask, a compass for finding the way, a torch and a whistle, and a first aid kit.

A fleece is a woolly jacket that can keep you warm on cold mountains. Mountain weather can change very quickly.

Trousers should be light and comfortable, neither too tight nor loose and flapping. Jeans are too heavy and wet when it rains, and too hot in warm countries.

A flysheet keeps the inner shell of the tent from becoming wet with dew.

Igloo-style tents are kept rigid with light, bendy plastic rods.

Walking boots should be strong but comfortable. They should support the ankle and have soles that will not slip.

Waterproof leggings may be worn in areas of bog and deep snow.

Camping skills are crucial for outdoor survival. In national parks and country regions you will only be able to camp at an approved site. But one day you might find yourself out on your own, camping in remote jungle or wilderness. Tents should be light to carry, and easy to put up. They should keep out wind and water. Pitch your tent in a sheltered spot, on flat ground which will not flood.

Hoods or hats should suit the climate. Hats with broad brims should protect the head in hot weather. Woollen hats keep the head warm and hoods keep out rain and snow.

The doorway zips up tightly to keep out the weather.

The groundsheet of this tent is fitted to the base, so water cannot seep in.

The envelope is the balloon's outer skin. It is normally made of nylon, or of other tough fabrics such as plastics or polythene.

Propane gas is stored as a liquid, inside metal cylinders in the gondola. It fuels the burners which heat the air inside the balloon.

Bags of sand are sometimes carried as ballast, weighting down the balloon. They can be released to make the balloon climb more quickly.

Hot air is normally used to raise balloons. Various other gases can sometimes be used, such as helium, hydrogen or methane.

The gondola is the part of the balloon that carries the passengers. It may be an open basket or a closed capsule.

UP INTO THE SKY

The huge flapping **balloon** is spread out on the ground. As it is filled with hot air, it swells out into a gigantic, colourful globe. Soon it rises above the countryside, high into the air. The buildings and roads far below become tiny. Can you bear to look down? The balloon is tugged by the wind and gathers speed. Balloons have no engines or propellers, so balloonists must study the patterns of winds and air currents along the route.

A rotary wing lifts the autogyro into the air up to a height of 3500 metres. It is powered by a small petrol engine.

Some autogyros have wheels, but this one has skids which are good for landing on snow. Most autogyros can carry two passengers.

The autogyro is very manoeuverable. This makes it ideal for exploring over difficult terrain like forests and jungles.

Gliders, hang-gliders, microlights, autogyros and even person-carrying kites can all help us fly like the birds and explore from above. Autogyros have a rotary wing like a helicopter for lift and a propeller like an aircraft for forward movement. They have small engines which can push them along at speeds of over 160 kilometres per hour.

WHITE WATER!

Rapids ahead! The flow of water speeds up as the river bed slopes downhill. Foaming water swirls around boulders. A normal boat would soon be smashed to pieces on the rocks. The explorer has two choices – a canoe or an inflatable raft. A really skilled canoeist can paddle and roll through the white water in a kayak. But an inflatable is bigger. It can bounce off rocks and carry more people and equipment.

The crew faces forward and back-paddles against the current.

Equipment must be kept in watertight containers and roped down behind the rowing deck.

Lifejackets must be worn at all times. Helmets protect the head from rocks. Gloves, trainers and wetsuits may also be worn.

White-water rafting and kayaking are popular sports, but to an explorer these may be the only ways of reaching a remote area. If big waterfalls lie ahead, then the boats will have to be 'portaged' – carried along the bank – or hauled through the river with ropes. If the explorer decides to run the rapids, then a plan must be agreed by the crew and all the equipment must be checked. Once the boat is in the water, it's too late for anyone to change their mind!

Inflatables vary in size. Some rivers will take giant rafts 12 metres long. Others need smaller craft about 4 metres long.

FACT BOX
If you are rafting in Africa, watch out for a hippo collision! The big animals can be very fierce and slash the air tubes with their sharp tusks.
Big inflatables carry tourists on the Colorado River through the world's deepest gorge, the Grand Canyon.

Air tubes keep the raft bouncy. The outer skin is made of a very tough nylon.

KICKING UP DUST

Deserts are a real challenge for explorers. These regions are dry and dusty, with few plants and animals apart from deadly scorpions or snakes. There are huge areas with no roads or towns and it may take days to reach the nearest water hole or oasis. It is easy to get lost. Fierce winds carry sand and grit, which can strip the paint from a truck and cover up roads. The only landmarks may be high dunes, heaps of sand which shift in the wind.

Cover your head! Explorers often copy desert peoples such as the Tuareg and the Bedouin who wear head cloths against the heat and dust.

Camels have thick eyelashes to keep out the sand and grit. They are perfectly equipped for desert survival.

Camels' nostrils are designed to filter out the dust.

Deserts include the hottest places on Earth, such as the Sahara in North Africa. Could you stand a temperature of 58°C? Deserts can also be bitterly cold places, and even the Sahara can be very chilly at night. Most desert vehicles need four-wheel drive, air filters, broad tyres and reserves of fuel. Equipment includes shovels for digging vehicles out of sand dunes, metal ladders to place across soft sand, and a compass for checking your position.

Motorbikes can be used as desert transport. They cross hard, gravelly deserts better than soft sand.

Bigger fuel tanks may need to be fitted for long journeys.

Panniers carry equipment and spare parts for the bike.

Various tyres can be fitted to suit the type of ground you are crossing. Gravel or thorns may cause punctures.

IN THE JUNGLE

Tall, leafy treetops block out the daylight. Moisture drips from the tangle of creepers and vines. Monkeys scream in the branches and snakes slither out of swamps. Welcome to the tropical rainforest! You may be able to ride ponies or mules in the forest, but more often you will have to travel on foot or by canoe along the rivers.

Deep in the jungle you might find a ruined city or an ancient statue covered in creepers.

Shirts must cover your arms to the wrist, to avoid insect bites.

Maps of the route can be wrapped in a clear plastic envelope and hung around the neck, so that they can be read easily.

The rainforest is hot and wet. You need to carry lightweight waterproofs. Drying out wet clothes is almost impossible. Creepy-crawly insects make it necessary to sleep off the ground, in a hammock. Always sleep under a mosquito net, as deadly illnesses such as malaria can be passed on to you by insect bites. During the day you can wear ointment to keep away the insects. For food you can catch fish or even snakes, but beware of poisonous berries and nuts.

Packs should include emergency rations, medicines, distress flares to attract rescue aircraft, tablets for purifying water and a compass.

All equipment must be waterproof, including field glasses, cameras and watches.

Jungle boots up to the knee will protect your legs against snakes, spiders and blood-sucking leeches.

ICE AND SNOW

White out! The whole landscape is covered with ice and snow. The wind howls, chilling you to the bone. These are the frozen lands around the North and South Poles, the coldest places on Earth. Temperatures in Antarctica have been known to drop to −89°C! And winds can make low temperatures seem even lower. Frostbite can freeze your flesh and make your fingers and face turn black and blue.

Huskies are tough dogs used by polar explorers. A team of 5 to 15 huskies may be used to pull one sled. Huskies can sleep peacefully through an overnight blizzard.

Goggles may be worn to protect the eyes from driving snow or stinging ice crystals. Sometimes the whiteness is so dazzling that it can blind you. Dark glasses must be worn.

Cross-country skis can be used for travelling over the ice and snow. A long journey can be very tiring.

Furs and skins are still often used to stay warm, but many modern waterproof materials are just as warm and are lighter to wear.

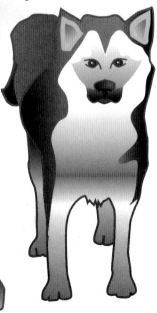

Mittens keep the hands warm and stop your fingers getting frostbite.

Polar expeditions normally take place in the brief summer, when the days are long and light and some of the ice covering the sea has melted. The Antarctic summer in the south takes place during the months of the Arctic winter in the north. The Inuit people, who live in the Arctic, used to build overnight shelters from blocks of frozen snow. These were called igloos. Today's polar explorers normally camp in tents.

Snowmobiles are a bit like motorbikes with runners instead of wheels. They are used all over the Arctic for travel and for hauling loads.

Supplies carried on the sled may include cooking stoves, food, medical supplies, a radio and scientific equipment.

ALONE AT SEA

Your ship has sunk a thousand kilometres from home. You have radioed for help and climbed into your life raft. You are all alone. Who will find you here in the middle of the ocean? Will you drown or be attacked by sharks? The waves are as big as houses and their crests are streaming with white spray. The sky is black and stormy.

Distress flares can be fired. These are rockets which climb high into the sky. They can be seen for miles around. Perhaps a ship or aircraft will spot them and come to the rescue.

The life raft will keep you alive even in rough seas. But you will need supplies of water and food.

FACT BOX
The 'roaring forties' is the name given to the waters of the far south, where northwesterly gales fill the sails of yachts but also pile up huge waves. The first person to sail solo around the world (1895-98) was an American called Captain Joshua Slocum. He couldn't swim!

you are tired, wet and hungry. Suddenly you hear the sound of shouting above the howl of the wind. Help is here! A yacht on a round-the-world race has heard your radio message and seen your distress flare. A line is thrown to your life raft. Soon you are safe and drinking hot chocolate in the galley.

Know your ropes and knots!
Ropes and lines are needed to make the yacht work properly, to stop the crew members being washed overboard – and to save shipwrecked sailors!

Waterproofs are worn from head to toe when the weather turns nasty.

CAVES AND POTHOLES

If you hate narrow, closed-in places, this is no place for you! You are inching your way along a narrow shaft, deep underground. Icy water is trickling down your neck and it is as dark as night. Sharp rocks graze your knuckles. But then the passage opens out into a vast cave, with crystals glittering from the rock face. All your hard work seems worthwhile!

Ropes clipped to harnesses help the caver descend into a shaft and to climb back out.

Helmets protect the head from dangerous bumps and knocks. They are fitted with lamps to show the way ahead.

Tough overalls are the best thing to wear underground.

FACT BOX
The proper name for a caver or potholer is a 'speleologist'.
The world's longest cave system is in Mammoth Cave National Park, Kentucky, where over 560 kilometres have been explored.
The world's deepest cave is the Jean Bernard Network in France, which goes down below 1,600 metres.

Cavers are always at risk from rock falls and from rising water levels, as rain sinks down from the surface. Injured cavers may have to be strapped to a stretcher before being hauled back to the surface. The caving team and their equipment must be organized with great attention to detail. Radio or telephone links may be used to call in the rescue services from the expedition's surface base.

People who explore caves may include geologists, historians in search of ancient burials or naturalists looking for bats or spiders. All will need their own special equipment.

Caves which are dry for most of the year may suddenly fill up with a surge of muddy water.

IN SEARCH OF THE UNKNOWN

Travellers sometimes tell extraordinary **tales**. Expeditions may have to set out to find if they are true. In many parts of the world there are stories of strange animals or people living in remote areas of forest or mountains. High in the Himalaya mountains there are tales of a weird, hairy creature called a Yeti. Climbers say they have seen its footprints in the snow.

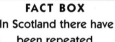

FACT BOX

In Scotland there have been repeated sightings over many years of an unknown monster in a lake called Loch Ness. Reports suggest that it looks rather like a long-necked dinosaur. Expeditions have scanned the whole lake but no monster has been found. Does it exist, or has the story been made up to attract visitors to the area?

Sometimes truth does turn out to be stranger than fiction. A fish called the coelacanth was caught off South Africa in 1938. Until then scientists had believed that the coelacanth became extinct 70 million years ago.

Food might attract a creature to the edge of the campsite. Could they be lured into a trap which wouldn't harm them?

In the Andes mountains of South America, people have seen strange, unknown creatures. In the wildernesses of North America backpackers have reported sightings of another shaggy being, the mysterious 'Bigfoot'. Are you going on a hunt for monsters? Keep quiet! Noise and chatter might drive shy creatures away. Look for strange tracks and footprints. Take field glasses and a camera.

Video- and audio-tape recorders are carried to record any evidence of strange creatures. What does a yeti look like? Does it have a call?

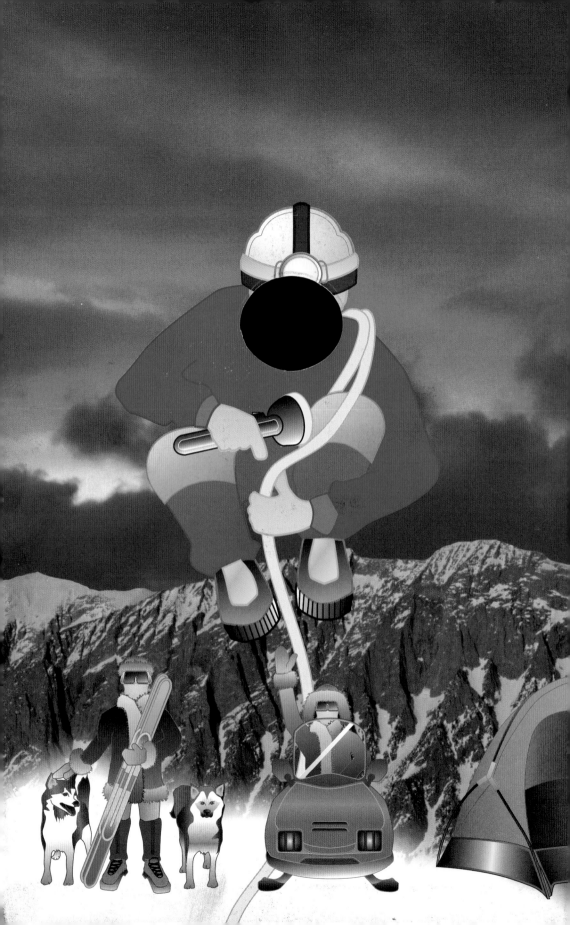